C000184669

Sprotbrough, Cadeby, Cusworth & Levitt Hagg

Until 1849 people communicating between Sprotbrough and Warmsworth crossed the River Don at Sprotbrough by means of a ferry. Thereafter, they used the bridge included in this view looking towards Warmsworth. The Toll House, also featured, is presently the home of Sprotborough artist Sheila Bury, and her picture framer husband Mike.

IMAGES OF ENGLAND

Sprotbrough, Cadeby, Cusworth & Levitt Hagg

Peter Tuffrey

NONSUCH

Boat Lane, Sprotbrough. The view is similar today with the exception of the corn miller's cottage in the distance, which has since been demolished.

First published 1997
This new pocket edition 2006
Images unchanged from first edition

Nonsuch Publishing Limited
The Mill, Brimscombe Port,
Stroud, Gloucestershire, GL5 2QG
www.nonsuch-publishing.com

Nonsuch Publishing is an imprint of Tempus Publishing Group

British Library Cataloguing in Publication Data.
A catalogue record for this book is available from the British Library.

ISBN 1-84588-319-5

Typesetting and origination by Nonsuch Publishing Limited
Printed in Great Britain by Oaklands Book Services Limited

Contents

A group of children enjoy having their picture taken in front of a Levitt Hagg beehive limekiln.

For Hugh Parkin.
Thanks for your help and encouragement.

Introduction

Four villages in the Doncaster area are included in this publication, all in close proximity to each other, though one - Levitt Hagg - was cleared during the late 1950s. The main, radical changes affecting the other three villages came when the estates to which they belonged were broken up. In 1925, following the Sprotbrough Estate sale, buildings, farms and areas of land were dispersed in Cadeby and Sprotbrough. Similarly, in 1952, changes occurred in Cusworth after the death of Robert Cecil Battie-Wrightson, the last Cusworth squire. However, a small portion of the Cusworth Estate remains intact, within the village itself, due to the establishment of the Cusworth Church Trust.

Many people have argued, and I count myself as one of them, that the demolition of Sprotbrough Hall and the sale of its many treasures was a sad loss to the area. The extent of the deficit may be appreciated while looking at the interior and exterior pictures of the Hall included here. Fortunately, Cusworth Hall has been saved, though its contents too, were dispersed. A glimpse of estate life, once so common place in the Doncaster area with its many country houses, is aptly portrayed in the set of Cusworth Hall staff pictures. For the use of these I have to thank W.H. Gordon-Smith, who is Agent to the Cusworth Church Trust.

The book's pictures themselves come from the cameras of quite a number of individuals, though, of course, those taken by noted local photographers such as Edgar Leonard Scrivens, J. Simonton & Son and Bagshaw & Son, stand out as fine examples of this art. Scrivens' set of the marriage of Miss Bewick Copley and Capt Foljambe on 16 November 1909 have a unique intimacy, almost making the onlooker feel as though they are part of the crowd witnessing the event.

The only hint of industry in the four areas is the quarrying in the Warmsworth Cliffs at Levitt Hagg. Many aspects of this work are shown in the photographs, capturing the true community spirit which, I'm sure, once existed there. The Levitt Hagg pictures were mainly gleaned from Hugh Parkin who has devoted much of his time over the last fifteen years to collecting material on the area and giving illustrated informative talks about it. He is also very active at Sprotbrough Flash Nature Reserve.

While there has been little industry in the four areas, pubs have also been scarce. Levitt Hagg and Cusworth have always been 'dry' villages. Cadeby did not have its own pub until 1975, while Sprotbrough, at one time, was without a watering hole for nearly a century. Although it was disappointing that my appeal in the local press and on Radio Sheffield for pictures and information on Fowler's small factory at Sprotbrough was unfruitful, I hope, nevertheless, that this publication may encourage someone somewhere to unearth material which will obviously be of use to other authors in future.

The photographs also reveal other aspects of the area, including the number of changes occurring along the River Don during the present century. Bridges have been built or rebuilt; the river's course at Sprotbrough has been altered; features like the two mills along the banks have disappeared, while other noted structures have fallen into disrepair, including Sir Godfrey Copley's engine house. Personally, I am pleased that in recent years the Don Gorge, scything through several of the areas illustrated, has been recognised as a stretch of natural beauty, with a section - Sprotbrough Flash - becoming a nature reserve. Long may it flourish.

Finally, I would like to acknowledge the help given by W.H. Gordon-Smith and Albert Warrender.

Peter Tuffrey
April 1997

One

Rambling Round

It is thought that the barn pictured here on Anchorage Lane, Sprotbrough, was built in the seventeenth century from the stones of the original Hospital of St Edmund and Ancres House, which occupied a site nearby. In 1952 the site returned to the church. It was bought by the diocese of Sheffield and dedicated as the Centre of St Edmund in February 1954. The Guides, Scouts, Cub Scouts, Brownies and Church Lads Brigade have all used the church hall enclosed in the thick walls of the former barn.

Main Street, Cadeby, looking west. For much of its existence the village, containing a number of good, typical seventeenth century farmhouses, belonged to the Sprotbrough estate. Property and land in Cadeby were included in the 1925 Sprotbrough Estate sale.

Main Street, Cadeby, looking east. The Revd Fardell in *Sprotbrough* (1850) said that '[Cadeby is] a well conducted, clean and healthy township', although it has been noted that soon afterwards, 'the Copleys thought it advisable to erect there a police house complete with lock-up'. On the right, with its gable end to the street, is a seventeenth century cement-rendered cottage.

Main Street, Cadeby, facing east. In recent times Cadeby has become an exclusive commuter village, very few people being associated with its traditional links with farming.

View in Cusworth village, looking west towards Cusworth Hall. The house off-centre to the left is the coach house.

The area where deer are seen grazing in Cusworth Park, during the early part of the twentieth century, is presently occupied by a car park. According to W.H. Gordon-Smith in his book *Cusworth Hall and the Battie-Wrightson Family* (1990), 'Deer remained at Cusworth until the Second World War when they all disappeared one night after the park gates were left open'.

Stonemason's cottage at Cusworth, looking north. In *Rambles Round Doncaster* (1994), W.H. Gordon-Smith stated that 'The Hall dominated Cusworth and almost everybody in the village worked for the Estate. On entering the village, you couldn't help but notice that it was dense with trees. In winter there was the wonderful smell of burning logs emitting from the cottage chimneys... even with the infilling of a few modern properties in large gardens, the old Cusworth village still has the air of a private country estate'.

Scene in Cusworth village. The buildings include Church Cottage (formerly the bothy) and Cusworth Glebe (the head gardener's house). Interestingly, it is considered that the latter two buildings stand on the former site of the original Cusworth Hall, built for the Wray family around 1583.

Above: From a bedroom window of Cusworth Manor House, we have a bird's eye view of Cusworth Estate buildings, occupying the fomer site of the old Elizabethan Cusworth Hall. The cart shed on the left eventually became the Battie-Wrightson Memorial Hall. Other buildings include the head gardener's house (now Cusworth Glebe), the bothy (Church Cottage), and the coach house. The old joiner's shop, brewery and stables in the distance have since been demolished.

Opposite below: Part of Levitt Hagg village is seen from the north side of the River Don. On the left is the Mission Hall/Reading Room, built in 1878. At one time, the first house in the middle of the row of houses in the centre belonged to William Chester and the last house, in the same row, to J. Hallgate.

View of the River Don near Levitt Hagg, looking east. Levitt Hagg was situated in the gorge where the lower magnesian limestone is exposed in Warmworth Cliffs. John Battie began quarrying operations at the base of the Warmsworth Cliffs in the 1750s. He had entered the quarrying business because the growth in population in the eighteenth century created a demand for stone to build more houses. The increase in population also led to higher food prices and a need for more food growing areas. This in turn initiated the establishment of lime burning at the quarries, as lime was essential in the reclamation of marginal land for agriculture. On the right is the house known as No. 1 Levitt Hagg. Note also the boat building taking place near the property. The first boat to be built in the area was completed around 1868. This was carried out by the quarrying company of Lockwood, Blagden & Crawshaw.

During the mid-eighteenth century, Levitt Hagg was adopted as the name for a dwelling house erected on part of the site of a clearing on the south bank of the River Don. Later, when more buildings were constructed and a small village was formed by the early nineteenth century, Levitt Hagg was used for the name of the whole settlement.

Boats moored along the River Don near Levitt Hagg, while work was being undertaken, in 1907, on straightening the canal near Sprotbrough. According to William Pierson in his article *Levitt Hagg – A Deserted Quarrying Hamlet*, 'The later Yorkshire (or Humber) Keel was a craft well suited not only to the task of navigating narrow shallow rivers, but also the exposed estuary of the Humber. Occasionally, they ventured along the coast... In narrow, or dangerous sections of the canal or river, and in the absence of wind, the keel reefed her sails and was towed by a horse'.

Looking eastwards at Levitt Hagg, with a group of six cottages known as White Row on the right. These were constructed by Messrs Lockwood, Blagden & Crawshaw around 1815. Each of the cottages contained one living room, two bedrooms and a pantry beneath the staircase. Outside was a coal house, an earth closet and a wash house. Water was obtained from wells nearby.

Levitt Hagg, facing west. The origin of the name Levitt Hagg is uncertain, but if both words are examined individually, a conclusion may be drawn. The first word is possibly derived from the surname Levett or Levytt. Thomas Levett had land in High Melton and Wildthorpe in the sixteenth and seventeenth centuries and the altar tomb near the pulpit in Sprotbrough church is the memorial to the family of William Levytt. The second word is perhaps easier to interpret, since 'hagg' is an Anglo-Saxon term meaning clearing. Whether the 'hagg' or clearing below the Warmsworth Cliffs was in some way connected with the Levett or Levytt families remains uncertain, but it is tempting to suggest this might have been the case, and thus the name Levitt Hagg.

A view of the Mission Hall and Nos 6 to 9 Levitt Hagg, from the north side of the River Don. The Mission Hall was designed by J. Demaine of York and could accommodate 180. At the turn of the century services were conducted by the Warmsworth Rector or his curate. To ensure safety from quarrying operations, the Levitt Hagg houses were built as far away from the Warmsworth Cliffs as possible. However, as the cliffs were initially only 200 yards away from the waterside, the buildings were situated along the river bank.

A closer view of Nos 6 to 9 Levitt Hagg. The man with the 'begging' dogs is George Chester, who lived at No. 6. In the window of his house a 'Tea' sign is displayed. George was also noted for keeping bees in his garden. Many cottagers kept hens or pigs and, together with villagers at Warmsworth, the two communites formed a pig club. W. Pierson (*op. cit.*) mentions that, 'Each member paid one penny a week and anyone losing an animal was compensated; the balance at the end of the year was distributed amongst members'. At the time the picture was taken, Mr and Mrs Issitt occupied No. 7, Mr and Mrs W. Chester (jnr) No. 8, and Mr and Mrs J. Hallgate No. 9.

Joe Kellett (right) walking with youngsters Stephen Day and Linda Commerson at Levitt Hagg. During the early years of the twentieth century there were twenty-one houses, populated by around 100 people. The community operated a sick club, each member paying 6d monthly. Sick pay of 10s weekly was paid for a limited period.

Alan Barker in a rowing boat on the River Don near Levitt Hagg. Later, Alan lost his sight, moving to Sprotbrough where he bought a newsagent's business. His disability did not stop him delivering newspapers around High Melton, Cadeby and Sprotbrough, retiring in January 1978. The background includes the Mission Hall and Nos 6 to 9. At one time the Reading Room was partitioned from the Mission by a screen though around the time of the First World War, it was converted for use as a house.

Balby-based photgraphers J. Simonton and Son were responsible for taking this picture, featuring White Row (Nos 14 to 19), some 'navigation' stables, Nos 20 and 21, and four beehive kilns. A report of the County Medical Officer upon the sanitary condition of the Doncaster Union in 1925, highlighted that the Levitt Hagg houses most in need of repair were the White Row cottages, the first to be demolished in 1940.

A group of Levitt Hagg folk pictured with a shipment of coal. The shipment was delivered annually for the villagers and unloaded by them after work. The workers paid for the coal via a weekly deduction from their wages.Coal for firing the lime kilns was shipped from pits along the the Don Valley. Cargoes of stone and lime were being moved by road and rail by the 1930s, the river trade being finished by 1940.

Right: Mrs Kellett captured outside her house, No. 18 White Row, Levitt Hagg, *c.* 1908. Cottages in White Row contained one living room, a pantry under the stairs and two bedrooms. The properties lacked a sink, cupboards, water or proper sanitation. W. Pierson, recalls, 'The women (of Levitt Hagg) usually shopped one day a week in Doncaster, to reach which they walked to Balby where they were able to take the horse bus to the Hodgson and Hepworth Stores; on Saturdays, the bus came to the top of Mill Hill'.

Below: Another view taken by J. Simonton & Son of Levitt Hagg, looking east towards Sprotbrough. By 1860 the lime burning side of the business at Levitt Hagg was flourishing. Several cargoes were distributed by boat each week and the development of the railways created new markets, especially in Lancashire. To cope with new trade in this area the company established a lime depot in Manchester.

31. The Lime Quarries Levitt Hagg. J.S.&S.

Two quarry workers pose for the camera in the Warmsworth Cliffs, formed 230 million years ago at Levitt Hagg. As quarrying is a hazardous occupation, the community at Levitt Hagg often witnessed a number of serious and sometimes fatal accidents. Many were recorded throughout the nineteenth century, with the Victorian predilection for gory detail, in the *Doncaster Gazette*. The fire holes near the base of the 'face' of the rock in the picture are entrances to a passage which has been excavated from one side to the other, a length of about 60 ft. Its width is about 7 ft and height slightly more than 5 ft. The height of the 'face' of the rock is over 100 ft. The pillars between the entrances are left as supports; these have holes drilled in them into which charges of gelignite were inserted.

The lime kilns at Levitt Hagg, pictured around 1972. Lime burning ceased in the 1950s. The poor conditions and the seriously polluted state of the river led inevitably to all the houses at Levitt Hagg being condemned as unfit for occupation. A clearance order was issued by the Doncaster RDC on 25 May 1957 for the removal of dwellings numbered 1-13, as well as the derelict Mission Room. The notice was posted on 6 June 1957.

Two views of the quarry at Levitt Hagg. After the Second World War the introduction of modern plant and machinery caused the quarrying company to reduce the workforce.

Left: Number 5 Levitt Hagg with Mrs Lewis and her daughter proudly posing outside the property.

Below: The still waters of the River Don perfectly reflect the scene at Levitt Hagg, looking west. A large amount of the quarry company's output was distributed by boat, but when the South Yorkshire Railway Company's line was extended through the Warmsworth Cliffs in 1849, it enabled a considerable proportion of the stone and lime to be conveyed by rail. On the extreme right is the church, now disappeared, like all of the buildings.

In 1868 the first of three boats built by Lockwood, Blagden & Crawshaw was launched. However, boat building was not a major concern, the company's carpenters undertaking the work whenever their other commitments allowed them to do so. Number 1 Levitt Hagg can be clearly seen at the centre of this picture.

The blacksmith's shop at Levitt Hagg, c. 1900. During the early part of the twentieth century the male members of the Levitt Hagg community, after working more than 50 hours per week in the quarries or in associated jobs, mainly spent their time looking after their allotments or animals. Some frequented the Mission Hall/Reading Room, while others were attracted to cricket at Warmsworth.

Mrs T. Watson and her two children, Evelyn and Wilf, posing outside their house at Levitt Hagg. On the left, a joiner's workshop is attached to the house.

Another view of No. 1 Levitt Hagg, facing east. The blacksmith's shop is on the right and the woodmen's steaming shed on the left.

Sprotbrough Main Street. The old clock works (now in Cusworth Museum) once operated both the interior and exterior dials. The exterior dial in the tower now has an electrical movement. The old stone-built mounting steps on the right, near the entrance to the churchyard, would assist riders to mount or dismount from a horse in times gone by.

Main Street, Sprotbrough, looking eastwards.

Main Street, Sprotbrough, facing the church, with the Estate House, dating from the Victorian period, off centre to the right.

Main Street, Sprotbrough, at the junction with New Lane, looking eastwards. The chestnut tree, to the left, is on the site of the present Sprotborough Parish Club.

A group of cottages at Sprotbrough Boat, once part of the Copley Estate. Moving westwards, the road now leads to Sprotbrough Flash. Until the 1980s, whenever there was heavy rain in Sheffield or snow on the Pennines, water eventually crept up to the doorsteps of these cottages which overlook the River Don and canal. The problem was the water table. When there was a sudden rise in the level, the water shot up through the drains and through the field in front of the cottages.

Rambler's Cottage, Main Street, Sprotbrough. The village pump can be seen at the centre of the picture.

A group of cottages at Sprotbrough Boat. Note how the property on the right has been rebuilt (about 1912) since the photograph on the previous page was taken. The Revd Fardell in his *Sprotbrough* (1850), notes the following, 'The cottages of the poor, some having been rebuilt, are replete with the comforts and necessaries of that station in life'.

Cottages at Sprotbrough Boat, looking towards the corn mill, c. 1920. The house on the left is known as Tower Cottage.

Cottages at Sprotbrough Boat, looking westwards, *c.* 1895. The pair on the left were demolished in the 1920s.

The chancel at Sprotbrough's St Mary's church is thought to date from the late thirteenth century, but the west tower from around 1474 and the porch from 1632. Fragments of a Saxon cross shaft are incorporated in the south wall of the chancel.

Sprotbrough village, looking west. An idea of how some of the Sprotbrough village cottages appeared during the early nineteenth century is given by J. Holland in his *Tour of the Don* (1837), 'An ascent of a quarter mile brings us to the village of Sprotbrough. The place has a pleasant aspect; most of the cottages are white washed and many of them are tastefully overhung in front with roses, pyracanthus, jasmine and other plants'.

A First World War cannon pictured on Sprotbrough village green. Whilst staying at the rectory as a teenager, Douglas Bader, along with a few friends, pushed the cannon down Boat Lane. The cannon was removed and taken for scrap at the start of the Second World War. In the background is the saddle shop of J. Goodman.

Above: Doncaster Road, Sprotbrough, looking towards the junction with Thorpe Lane, c. 1950.

Right: Two children pose for the camera at the entrance to Sprotbrough Park. Though an alleged Saxon stone is incorporated in a buttress by the priest's door, no church is recorded at 'Sproteburgh' in Domesday Book; St Mary's was built by an early Fitzwilliam in about 1170. The Norman transitional column and capital, behind the pulpit, is the sole relic.

View of Sprotbrough cricket ground from the church. The Sprotbrough Cricket Club was originally called the Sprotbrough and Cadeby Cricket Club and played at both villages before moving to the present ground around 100 years ago. The 'Cadeby' part was dropped in 1896. Early records show that the club boasted a membership of fifty-nine in 1886, a figure which included two ladies. Although Saturday is presently the established day for local cricket, in the late nineteenth century there appeared to be no specific day, with the club playing games on Saturdays, Tuesdays and Thursdays in 1889. Cricket in Sprotbrough was carefully nurtured in the twentieth century by the one-time landlord of the Ivanhoe Hotel, Joe Lumb, whose grandson Richard once played for Yorkshire.

Corner of Main Street/Thorpe Lane, August 1963, shortly before the row of four stone-built terraced houses was demolished. Some of the houses included two rooms up and down, together with a detached garden.

Sprotbrough village showing the post office, on the left, and Al Goodman's shop, selling tobacco and confectionery. In the 1925 Sprotbrough Estate sale catalogue, the post office was described as being one of a terrace of three stone-built and tiled cottages, containing two rooms up, and two down.

On the canal, showing the house adjacent to the Flint Mill. The latter was used as a fuller's mill between 1600 and 1700 and a flint mill from 1700 until 1895. A Mr Burton recalled some memories of activities at the mill in the *Doncaster Gazette* of 29 September 1935: 'The flint was ground in water and then dried; it was like flour and when loads of 300 tons had been accumulated they would be sent to Hull for shipment to Spain... The house used to belong to the Copleys'.

Ladies enjoying themselves on what must be a summer's day, judging by their dress, on Nursery Lane, with the Nursery Lane Bridge in the background.

This picture is reproduced from the 1925 Sprotbrough Estate sale catalogue, being described as lot 41: 'A valuable property well known as Sprotbrough Park, richly timbered and with a fine Elm Avenue, having a long frontage to the main Sprotbrough Road, from which it is protected by a broad belt of finely grown timber... Water is laid on from the Estate supply. This is one of the most attractive sites in the district and is ripe for development as a first class building estate'.

Two

Buildings, Bridges and other Architectural Features

The Cadeby church of St John, a chapel of ease, was erected from the designs by Sir George Gilbert Scott in 1856 by Sir Joseph William Copley, at a cost of £5,000. It is a building of stone in the Early English style, consisting of chancel, nave, and aisles, all under one roof, with a bell gable over the chancel arch. The church was closed around 1969 because of problems with the interior stonework, which crumbled, causing a thick dust to cover the inside of the building.

The gamekeeper's cottage at Cusworth, built in 1726.

The stone-built Dillicar House, Cusworth Lane, Cusworth, dates from 1891. It was called Dillicar because it stood opposite the Dillicar Fields and was occupied by the agent to the Cusworth Estate. The Cusworth Agents have included R.J. Whittingham and a Miss Brackenbury. The present one is W.H. Gordon-Smith.

Cusworth Hall's north-facing frontage. The Hall was designed by Rotherham mason and architect George Platt; two wings added later were the work of James Paine. In one of the wings was a private chapel, the altar piece containing a painting by Francis Hayman RA of the *Good Samaritan*.

Cusworth Hall's south front, pictured about 1907. The photograph shows the new dining room, just completed at that time, behind the chapel.

An engraving by Thomas Malton, dated 1788, showing Cusworth Hall from the lake. After William Wrightson's death in 1756, his successor, John Battie, employed Richard Woods (1716-1793) to lay out the grounds to the Hall.

The Mission Hall/Reading Room site was given in 1878 by Cusworth Estate owner W.B. Wrightson and funds to meet the construction costs were raised through donations and subscriptions. Sturdily built of the stone that was so plentiful nearby, the Levitt Hagg chapel nevertheless fell into ruin and disappeared when the community nearby left the area. The building, known by the bargees as the Levitt Hagg lighthouse, faced the canal and river. By the early part of the twentieth century, the building was occupied as a house. The track in front was once part of a popular Sunday walk.

Sprotbrough Rectory, pictured here in about 1870, was drastically altered in the 1840s and not rebuilt as previously thought; the building dates back approximately 400 years. From plans dated 1840, before the alterations took place, it is clear that doorways shown on the drawing have been bricked up, walls moved, and that roof woodwork of the building's original design is still in place but not in use. There are still four doors and frames on the third floor that are believed to be the originals. The present front entrance and hall used to be the library, and the present lounge and French windows used to be the front door and hallway.

The Rectory paddock was sold in the early 1960s; Orchard School is presently on the site. The Rectory Mews estate was sold in 1983 to builders. In the same year Trevor Miller purchased the Rectory from the church and saved it from demolition. He is presently hoping to prove a theory, put forward by noted local historian W.H. Gordon-Smith, and agent to the Old Cusworth Estate, that the Rectory is the original Sprotbrough Hall and that the owners had the new Sprotbrough Hall built, selling or giving up the old Hall to the church. The latter body then had the building drastically altered in the 1840s, it being too large for a rector.

A bazaar taking place in the Sprotbrough Hall grounds. The Hall, once the seat of the Bewicke-Copleys, was erected by Sir Godfrey Copley in the reign of Charles II. It was a spacious mansion built from stone, standing on an extensive and well-wooded lawn. It consisted of a centre and two wings in the Classic style, containing many stately apartments, a well stocked library and a valuable collection of pictures. The gardens and grounds were extensive, carefully planted and tastefully laid out.

Sprotbrough Hall's north front. *Country Life* of 11 February 1922 comments on the Hall's style: 'It is probable that Sir Godfrey Copley (who had spent some time in Paris) was not inspired by any particular specimen of French architecture, and the tradition that the house is a copy of a wing at Versailles cannot be corroborated by fact. No doubt Versailles brought home to the Yorkshireman's mind the grandeur of that style, but when he got back to his native county, little more than vague impressions would seem to have remained with him'.

Right: The entrance hall or gun room at Sprotbrough Hall. Other rooms included the staircase hall, the dining room, the ante room, the drawing room or gallery, the library and the boudoir. On the first floor there were eleven principal bed and dressing rooms and the billiard room. The second floor contained twenty-eight bed and dressing rooms and three bathrooms.

Below: The Hall, looking west at Sprotbrough Hall. Above the boldly moulded chimneypiece is a portrait of Sir Godfrey Copley MP, FRPS, painted by Kneller. *Country Life* (*op. cit.*) states that 'At the eastern end there is a charming derivative of the medieval and Tudor screen, in the form of an arch flanked by two flat-topped doorways, which gives on to the stairs. The carving is very restrained and fine, and two diminutive spandrels containing cupids' heads occupy the spaces above the arch, while panels with broken corners surmount the two doors'.

Left: Sprotbrough Hall south front. By the marriage of William, second son of John Copley, of Batley Esq., with Dorothy, daughter and co-heiress of Sir William Fitzwilliam, the Sprotbrough Estate, which had been in the Fitzwilliam family from the time of the Conquest or soon after, descended to the Copleys, in which family it continued in the male line for six generations, until, on the death of Sir Godfrey Copley in 1709, it descended to Catherine, his only surviving daughter and heir. She was married to Joseph, second son of Sir Walter Moyle of Balke, Cornwall, whose son, Joseph Moyle, on becoming heir to his grandfather took the name of Copley, thereby continuing the name for some time.

Below: Sprotbrough Hall, from a painting by Van Diest (1655-1704), engraved by Bernard Lens (1680-1740). Apart from politics, Sir Godfrey also found time to pursue his interest in hydrostatics, constructing a magnificent ornamental fountain in Sprotbrough Hall's grounds around 1703.

Sprotbrough Hall's north facing front. It was once said that 'The drawing-room is very elegant and is in three divisions, each separated by columns; its total length is 73 feet; its height is twenty-two feet. Upon the garden front there is a broad terrace, with a flight of steps heading to the gardens, laid out in a taste comfortable to the age when the house was erected, they are singularly beautiful and much admired'.

Sprotbrough Hall once boasted a fine collection of pictures including the *Head of a Jew Rabbi* by Rembrandt, *Five Beautiful Sea Views* by Vandevelde, *A Sea Piece* by Backhuysen, *Christ Praying on the Mount* by Raphael, and *Lord Strafford and his Secretary* by Vandyck.

Sprotbrough Hall was put up for auction in 1925, at Doncaster Guildhall, by Lord Cromwell because of the burden of double death duties – his mother having died in 1923 while the mourners were assembling for the funeral of his father. This brought an end to the domination of Sprotbrough by a few families. The Hall was sold for a mere £5,100. In 1926 it was demolished, the potential of Sprotbrough having been quickly recognised; development steadily got under way and the parkland was carved up into building plots.

Sprotbrough Hall viewed from the Warmsworth side of the river. Today, from this position, a section of the balustrade at the foot of the former Hall's garden is still discernible. When the Hall was put up for sale in 1925, it was suggested in the sale catalogue that the property was 'admirably suitable for Institutional, Scholastic or Public Purposes'. However, a year later, it was demolished.

Two views from what is thought to have been a garden fete at Sprotbrough Hall, taken during the early 1920s. Whilst all seemed well at that time, by 10 September 1926 the *Doncaster Gazette* was reporting that the 'Sprotbrough Hall estate, now a wilderness, ready for the miscellaneous builders' heaps that inevitably precede the erection of houses, will soon be nought but a memory to those who have lived within a stone's throw of the once stately old country residence recently demolished'.

Sir Godfrey Copley constructed a magnificent ornamental fountain in the Sprotbrough Hall grounds around 1703. This came about following a visit to the Duke of Devonshire's Chatsworth House where an Emperor Fountain boasted a 290 ft jet. At that time it was the second highest in the world. Despite engineering difficulties, Sir Godfrey was determined to produce a fountain comparable with that at Chatsworth. He designed a method of conveying water from a low position near the river through pipes uphill to a tank on the flat roof of Sprotbrough Hall. *Doncaster Evening Post* reporter Clive Jones is pictured in December 1971 among the remains of the old engine house, near Sprotbrough Lock.

Sir Godfrey's hydrostatic improvements around the Sprotbrough Estate led to one material comfort being added to the Hall: a bath. In a letter dated 1707 he wrote, 'I have succeeded past my expectations in making such a bath for pleasure and convenience as I think no one in the kingdom hath yer like'. The pool was 35 ft long and 16 ft across and could be filled by the water engine, seen here, in less than 5 hours. Until 1930, when the village came onto a water board supply, the engine was used to supply water to the village through stand pipes. When the Don became too polluted to drink, the engine was again used to pump up water from an artesian well discovered beneath its site.

Two views of the New Lodge, or North Lodge, Sprotbrough, standing at the junction of Melton Road and Park Drive. In the 1840s Sir Joseph William Copley, who succeeded to the Sprotbrough Estate on the death of his father in 1838, was making considerable improvements to it. Amongst other things he decided to construct was a new and additional carriage-way which passed through much of the park before reaching the Hall. A lodge was built and the entrance was embellished with a fine set of bronze gates supported by six carved stone pillars. The date of their construction is confirmed by the *Doncaster Gazette* of 26 January 1849, which stated that, 'The beautiful new lodge, which has recently been completed, is a fitting entrance to the Park'. Following the break up of the Sprotbrough Estate in the mid 1920s, the gates and pillars were removed and re-erected at the entrance to Warmsworth Cemetery in the late 1930s.

The first Scala Club on Thorpe Lane, Sprotbrough. Later, a larger club was built off Sprotbrough Road, near Newton Lane. It was there, during the 1960s, that a number of noted stars from the entertainment world appeared.

Sprotbrough Bridge, looking towards Sprotbrough, c. 1910, on what was perhaps a traffic-free Sunday.

Sprotbrough Bridge, looking along the picturesque tree-lined road towards Warmsworth. The Bridge Lodge (on the right) was described in the Sprotbrough Estate sale catalogue of 1925 as, 'occupying a delightful rural position at the Bridge Head, and adjoining Boat Lane. It is substantially built of dressed stone with a flat roof with projecting eaves, and contains Four rooms, Well of Water and Garden...'.

Sprotbrough Bridge looking towards Sprotbrough. I wonder if anyone can identify the figures?

Left: The flint mill, operating until 1895, was situated by the weir on its west front, obtaining power by means of a water wheel. The mill used to adjoin the weir but there was a channel lower down the river to the mill, large enough to accommodate a boat alongside the mill for loading purposes. The entrance has since been filled up, the course of the river having been altered. Recalling his flint mill memories in the *Gazette* of 29 September 1935, Arthur Burton said, 'Not many men were employed there – only about four workmen and the manager. The flint was ground by a great big stone which revolved. The mill itself was very strongly built; it had to be strong for the massive water wheel used to shake the building'.

Below: Young boys pose for the camera outside the Toll House, Sprotbrough. Until 1888, tolls were collected from this building for the repair and maintenance of the river and canal bridges.

THE BRIDGE, SPROTBROUGH

Ivanhoe House, or the former Ferryboat Inn, was renamed the Copley Arms (the Copley family coat of arms can be seen on the frontage) when it was re-built in the middle of the nineteenth century. It is said that the inn was closed after two drunken customers from Levitt Hagg fell into the river and drowned, leaving the village without a pub until the 1930s, when the Ivanhoe Hotel was erected. Later, the building became a farm, which by the early 1980s was abandoned and derelict. When a local solicitor initially proposed to convert the building into a pub in 1983 the Sub Committee of South Yorkshire County Council's Planning Committee said that it represented 'an inappropriate intrusion of commercial development into this quiet, attractive green belt location'. Nevertheless, the scheme went ahead and the pub opened during 1986.

The barns of Ivanhoe House, c. 1981, before the site was developed by a local businessman, Peter Edwards. (Photograph by L. Bailey)

Above: In *Sprotbrough in History Part Two* (1969) it is stated that, 'The steady flow of new residents to Sprotbrough (during the mid 1920s) included several Methodist families; and there began in 1928, fortnightly meetings in Mr Spink's cottage near the church'. Several years later members moved to the Granary Meeting House, at the rear of Park House, pictured here during the 1930s. *Below:* Sprotbrough pump in a stone alcove in Main Street. The pump stands beneath an impressive coat of arms. The shield includes the Copley, Moyle and Pelham Arms.

The water of the Don powered mills at Sprotbrough for more than 700 years, the first reference being in a charter of 1279. There was a walk or fulling mill (where cloth was prepared between 1600-1700) and, later, this became a flint mill, where burnt flints were ground to powder for mixing with clay at the Don Pottery at Swinton, manufacturing earthenware. Seen here is the Flint Mill House in ruins.

Part of Sprotbrough village, looking west. The building on the right, once known as Shires Farm, later became Shires Stores. Once part of the Sprotbrough Estate, it was described in the 1925 sale catalogue as 'suitable for a gentleman's occupation, situated in a Pretty Garden, is stone built and slated and contains Four Bedrooms, Two Box Rooms, Two Garrets, Bath Room (h. and c.) and WC, Dining Room, Drawing Room, Sitting Room, Two Kitchens, Dairy and Pantry'.

The Manor Farm, Sprotbrough, described in the 1925 sale catalogue as, 'having long frontages to the High Melton Road, Spring Lane and to the River Don, extending in all to about 169 acres 1 rood 16 paces mostly on a gentle southern slope. The superior house situated in Sprot-brough village, is substantially built of stone with slated roof, and contains seven bedrooms'.

Anchorage House, situated at the fork of the Sprotbrough Road and Anchorage Lane, is a substantially-built red brick house with a tiled roof, including four bedrooms, box room, bathroom, dining room, drawing room, breakfast room, kitchen and pantry.

Newton Farm, having frontages to Sprotbrough Road and to Newton Lane, was bounded on the north by Cusworth Park and on the south by the River Don. Details in the 1925 sale catalogue noted that, '{It is} approached along Newton Lane, is stone built, cement-faced and tiled, contains six bedrooms...' At that time it was let to a Mr H.H. Bailey with other lands 'on a Yearly Candlemas Tenancy'.

The lock-keeper's cottage at Sprotbrough where, during times of bad flooding, it was reported that the keeper's bed floated to the bedroom ceiling! The worst floods in the area in the twentieth century occurred in 1932 and 1947.

Around 1848 the ferry boat was superceded by a bridge with a decorative cast iron span over the river. One was also built in stone over the canal. At the centre of each bridge were massive coats of arms in bold relief, one of which is shown here. The bridge work was supervised by Sir Joseph William Copley and it has been stated (W.E.A. 1969) that during his forty-five year span, 'he probably did more for the (Sprotbrough) village than any predecessor – with the possible exception of Sir Godfrey (Copley)'.

The first Sprotbrough Station was sited in Warmsworth cutting. The second station is pictured here looking west. The line, running through Sprotbrough from Denaby to Wrangbook junction (and then ultimately to Hull), was opened for goods traffic on 1 December 1894. There were two passenger trains a day in each direction. Sprotbrough Station was provided with a large waiting room, booking office and ladies and gents toilets. Passenger sevices ceased on 2 February 1903; goods services continued until 7 August 1967. Thereafter, the railway track was up-rooted.

Interior of Sprotbrough church, prior to major restoration work taking place in 1914/15, when the chancel was restored and the pulpit altered, re-using the sixteenth or seventeenth-century carved panels. The east end of the nave was also re-pewed, sixteenth-century carved panels from the previous box pews being incorporated. The Sprotbrough Hall pew in the south aisle was dismantled and a memorial chapel, enclosed by an oak screen, substituted.

In 1973, the *Doncaster Evening Post* reported that as part of European Architectural Heritage Year, the South Yorkshire County Council was to restore the historical lime kilns at Levitt Hagg. The remains of the lime kilns are being looked into here by Donald Clark (right) and Alan Sculthorpe. In J. Holland's *Tour of the Don* (1837) the following is mentioned in relation to the Levitt Hagg kilns: 'Some of the stone from the quarry is of a quality suitable for building purposes but for the most part is too soft for durable masonry and it is largely burned for lime in kilns near the riverside, taking full advantage of the situation for receiving coke, and for removing the lime or limestone by means of boats on the river. The kilns, which consist of rectangular masses of walling, about 6 ft high, with circular receptacles for the materials and a fire grate beneath, are filled with alternate layers of stone and coke with a little small coke on top. The fire is usually kept up three days and nights'.

The old wood and cast iron ornamental Sprotbrough Bridge over the River Don was replaced in 1897 by the one depicted below. The original bridge, built in the Grecian style and replacing the ferry, was 300 ft long, including seven arches, three of which were on each bank. The central arch was 100 ft in length.

The new steel girder Sprotbrough Bridge pictured shortly after completion; remains of the old one can be seen on the right hand side bank.

St Chad's caves at Sprotbrough, situated about 200 yards on the south side of Sprotbrough Bridge.

The remains of the old engine house in the wood opposite Sprotbrough Lock. The engine house was built by Sir Godfrey Copley in about 1703, a water wheel and pump raising water to a tank on the roof of Sprotbrough Hall. That was the domestic supply to the Hall; water was also provided for the fountains, an open air swimming pool and the village. In the post-war years, the engine house has been heavily vandalised, destroying a relic of a bygone age.

The substantial lattice girder bridge carrying the Doncaster Avoiding Line, opened in 1910, over the River Don at Sprotbrough. The purpose of the new line was to divert a portion of the traffic passing through Doncaster so as to relieve the congestion. The bridge has a central span of 163ft 7in in length, and three side spans of 52ft 4in each. The height of the central span above the level of the river is 42ft.

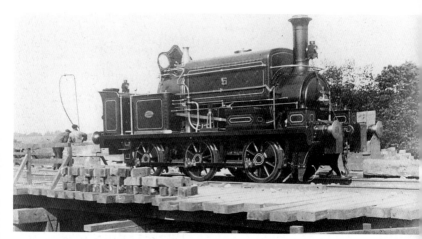

A unique picture illustrating one of the contractor's locomotives used during the building of the Avoiding Line.

When these pictures were taken during 1978, Sprotbrough Bridge was closed, undergoing major renovation work. To cross the river pedestrians were provided with a temporary footbridge – a cat-walk type structure of scaffolding and planks at the side of the main bridge. Meanwhile, on the bridge itself, all the surface material of the roadway was removed, exposing the tops of the masonry arches on the two approaches to the main steel span of the bridge. The arches were re-saddled with concrete, the whole thing waterproofed and the surface material replaced. The £40,000 scheme took about three weeks to complete.

Heavy iron gates once restricted access to Sprotbrough village on the north side of the canal bridge. They can be seen here in another view of the bridge taken during the early part of the twentieth century, as a horse and cart wends its way over. Note that the figure on the right has a penny farthing bicycle.

Figures musing by the Sprotbrough Corn Mill, (out of view), c. 1920. The stone bridge was replaced by a steel structure in 1934.

Three

Down by the River Don

The River Don was navigable, with difficulty, in the Middle Ages though it was not until the eighteenth century that measures were taken to make river transport more feasible. In 1726 an act was passed for making the river navigable from Doncaster to Tinsley, followed a year later by a similar act dealing with the lower reaches of the river. The two undertakings were merged in 1731. The head of navigation reached Aldwarke in 1733, Rotherham in 1740 and Tinsley in 1751, at total cost of £45,000. A scheme to extend the navigation to Sheffield was passed in 1815.

In 1850 the Don Navigation and its subsidiaries were taken over by the South Yorkshire Railway. The Navigation declined under railway control, with traffic and income falling and little being spent on maintenance. Through an act of 1889, the Navigation was transferred to the Sheffield & South Yorkshire Navigation Co. which had plans to make navigation to Sheffield possible for vessels up to 400 tons. These aims were never realised and traffic continued to decline. The view above was taken at Sprotbrough.

Keel passing Sprotbrough corn mill, the latter being demolished in 1932. This picturesque area was a natural attraction for artists and photographers alike.

Oarsman on the River Don at Sprotbrough, c. 1890. Note the old Sprotbrough 'river' bridge in the background.

Two views showing the Lock House during the 1960s.

The stone building in the middle distance on the right is a boat house. The picture was taken during the winter of 1963.

In the heyday of the Navigation, the typical boat used was the Humber Keel, a large bluff bowed barge with a single mast and square sail. These were either sailed or hauled by men until 1762 when the towpath, or 'hauling bank' was adapted for horse haulage. Companies of 'horse marines' used heavy horses to tow the barges. Steam power was introduced in the 1880s although some boats were not converted until after the turn of the twentieth century.

A keel on the River Don at Sprotbrough, looking towards the Lock House.

A scenic view including the corn mill at Sprotbrough, *c.* 1900.

A view at the turn of the twentieth century of the lock and lock house, Sprotbrough, from above Engine Wood. The pitch-roofed building, off centre to the right, is Sir Godfrey Copley's water pump.

Boating on the River Don at Sprotbrough was obviously once a favourite pastime, illustrated by these two photographs taken in about 1920. Boats were hired from either Hexthorpe or Conisbrough, depending on whether boaters wished to travel up or down stream.

The *Robert E. Lee* is seen sailing here at Levitt Hagg. It was built by the Barker brothers and a Mr Kellett of Levitt Hagg.

A keel threads its way past the corn mill at Sprotbrough, c. 1910. Note that the sail is being lowered in preparation for the vessel to pass underneath Sprotbrough Bridge.

Cameramen setting up their equipment to capture the picturesque views to be found at Sprotbrough during the early years of the twentieth century.

A boat full of people pictured near the mill at Sprotbrough. The large number of children present, together with a soldier in uniform, may suggest this was a Sunday school trip during the First World War. They were probably on their way to Levitt Hagg. The introduction of the Waterbus Service in 1976 gave the opportunity to thousands of people to partake once again in the pleasures of water travel along the River Don and the South Yorkshire Navigation. In 1978 over 14,000 tickets were sold.

A horse takes its feed on the tow path near Sprotbrough corn mill while, presumably, hauling the keel, c. 1900.

A splendid picture of *The Beverley*, with sail being lowered while passing Sprotbrough corn mill, c. 1900.

Two views looking over to Warmsworth Cliffs and Levitt Hagg from Sprotbrough Boat. This picture was probably taken *c*. 1905, two years before the canal was straightened.

This view was probably taken around 1910.

View at Sprotbrough, *c.* 1950, showing the new metal bridge over the canal and the old corn miller's cottage, now the site of a car park.

Above the falls at Sprotbrough, *c.* 1930. Fish were still present in the river at this time, but it was dead between 1940 and the 1980s. Today, the river is clean and angling matches take place along its banks most weekends.

Work taking place at Sprotbrough Lock during early spring, 1980.

On 26 November 1980, Sprotbrough Lock, the first in the improvement scheme to be built to 700 ton barge standard, was officially opened. Throughout the construction of the lock, completed in 11 months at a cost of £98,000, traffic continued to navigate, apart from a 12 day interruption when the old lock was cleared away. In the picture below Sir Frank Price (left), Chairman of British Waterways Board, receives a framed address from Cllr Joe Brough, Chairman of the South Yorkshire County Council. The address recorded the payment of a substantial instalment by South Yorkshire County Council towards their commitment to contribute £1 million to the overall cost of the South Yorkshire Canal Improvement Scheme.

A push/tow barge train of three craft, loaded with 280 tons of steel, passing through Sprotbrough Lock.

Vehicles being hauled from the River Don after being dumped by joy riders, c. 1982.

Right: During February 1990, a specially-built
55 ft narrow boat named *Sprotbrough Painter* was
launched into the South Yorkshire Navigation
at Doncaster for Sprotbrough-based watercolour
artist Sheila Bury. She has used the boat as
a floating studio, touring the region drawing
waterway scenes. At the time a spokesman for
British Waterways, John Nuttall said, 'We fully
support Sheila in her work. We hope it will
help promote the beauty of the waterways'.
Photographs by Hugh Parkin.

Below: The boat was built by R.B. Fabrications,
Ollerton, and fitted out by Sheila's husband Mike.

A wharf was constructed at Steetley's Cadeby Quarry in 1982 and stone is still being moved from there today by Alan Oliver. Cadeby stone has been used at York Minster, the Bank of England and the Houses of Parliament, as well as for road and canal repairs.

Four

Events

Lady Isabella Battie-Wrightson (centre) as Britannia at Cusworth Hall. W.H. Gordon-Smith (*op. cit.*) states, 'Lady Isabella was well known for her fancy dress parties... Everyone on the Estate took part – even the agent and the village children'.

Lady Isabella Battie-Wrightson (centre) as Britannia at Cusworth Hall. These parties invariably took place in the new dining room. Lady Isabella Georgiana Katherine Cecil was the eldest daughter of William Alleyne Cecil, third Marquis of Exeter of Burghley House, Stamford. She married William Henry Thomas (who took the name of Wrightson by Royal Licence), in London on 7 August 1884. William Henry died in 1903.

Lady Isabella pictured at Cusworth Hall on the north front steps with the bandsmen and entire complement of the 5th Battalion KOYLI. Her son Robert can be seen on the front row, first left, with a sword over his right shoulder.

Trying to cope with the floods at Levitt Hagg during the 1930s. Being so close to the river, the area sometimes experienced serious flooding, coupled with contamination of drinking water in the wells. At one point, water was carried by cart from another district.

Floods at Levitt Hagg in 1932. The two men in the foreground are Wilf and Cyril Watson.

Retrieving a steam traction engine which has fallen into the River Don at Levitt Hagg, *c.* 1926.

An ex-War Department steam traction engine pictured after being hauled from the River Don at Levitt Hagg, c. 1926.

Sprotbrough villagers line up on 16 November 1909 when Gladys Bewicke-Copley married Major Hubert Francis Fitzwilliam Brabazon Foljambe, of the King's Royal Rifles, third son of the Rt Hon F.J.S. Foljambe of Osberton, Worksop. Major Foljambe was one of the first to fall in the war, news of his death arriving in September 1914.

Left: Wedding day scenes in Sprotbrough on 16 November 1909.

Below: Guests arriving at Sprotbrough Hall for the wedding of Miss Bewicke Copley and Capt Foljambe on 16 November 1909.

E.L.S.5. MARRIAGE OF MISS BEWICKE COPLEY AND CAPT FOLJAMBE AT SPROTBROUGH. NOVR 16TH 1909.

Scene at Sprotbrough War Memorial, *c.* 1920s.

Scene at the opening of the new Sprotbrough Road Methodist church on 4 March 1939.
An adjoining Sunday school was erected in 1962 and, five years later, a fine wrought iron
communion rail was installed, being made by Conisbrough Northcliffe School students. Those
depicted include Mr Revill, Mrs Lambert, Revd Swansbrough, Mr Dudley and Mr Scargill.

Maypole scene at Sprotbrough Hall. Those holding the maypole ribbons include Jack Short, Alice Holt, Edith Triby, Ron Short, Mabel Watson, Edith Cole, Alan Hopkins.

Flood scene at Sprotbrough Lock during 1932.

Military parade at Cusworth Hall, facing north. Lady Isabella is pictured second on the right; her son Robert Cecil is fourth.

Hexthorpe Cubs, in the foreground, watching the haystack fire at Levitt Hagg in 1920. At this time the Cub mistress was Miss Goodchild.

Group at the Sprotbrough camp ground, near the old Flint Mill house.

The camp at Sprotbrough on Whit Monday 1914. This field is between the river and the 'bends' on the road to Warmsworth.

The Camp, Whit-Monday 1914.   H.M.S.

Another view of the camp at Sprotbrough on Whit Monday 1914.

The Camping Ground. Sprotboro. J.S.&S.

The camping ground at Sprotbrough.

Floods at Sprotbrough during 1947.

A Yorkshire Traction Co. motorbus slowly makes its way through the floods on Sprotbrough Road.

Five

Groups and Portraits

Group of figures outside Bourne Cottage at Cadeby.

Visit of Sprotbrough Copley Middle School children to Cadeby Quarry on 27 April 1994.
Photographs by Hugh Parkin.

Above: Pictured in his 'open air' studio at Cadeby Quarry is sculptor Michael Disley of Rotherham. He carved the musicians on the front of Sheffield's Leadmill.
Photograph by Hugh Parkin.

Right: Robert Cecil Battie-Wrightson, of Cusworth Hall, who was born on 24 April 1888. When he was aged 19 his mother bought him a commission in the 5th Battalion of The King's Own Yorkshire Light Infantry, serving as a Lieutenant until 1912. He married Louie Evelyn Lupton in 1914, though after a few years they were separated. During the First World War Robert Cecil served in the Royal Army Service Corps. Afterwards, he lived at Cusworth with Christabel Bentley. He died aged 63 in 1952, the last Cusworth Hall squire.

A group of the Cusworth Hall staff, *c.* 1940s, including Fred Wright, Gertie Myers and Marie Chambers. Gertie Myers lived at the Cusworth Lodge and during her employment at the Hall was a maid and then the cook.

The Cusworth Estate gamekeeper Fred Wright, his wife, mother-in-law and two daughters Alice and Mabel, pose for the camera outside their appropriately titled gamekeeper's cottage. Alison Morrish in her book *Caring For Cusworth* (no date) states that, 'The gamekeeper could provide rooks and pigeons for pies'.

Two chambermaids lean from the south front breakfast room/morning room window at Cusworth Hall.

Pictured in the late 1920s, outside the Cusworth Hall's north front are gamekeeper Fred Wright, Muriel Shaw (left) and Phyllis Lawton.

Cusworth Hall groundsman Bill Meadows, pictured with a delivery van during the late 1920s.

Christabel Bentley, front row left, is grouped with the Cusworth Hall staff around 1939.

Left: Three chambermaids, including Clara Farr and Muriel Shaw, frolicking in the Cusworth Hall duck pond. *Right:* A Cusworth Hall butler is seen beneath the office window on the north front.

Bill Meadows, Cusworth Hall's groundsman and driver between 1925-28, is mowing the lawn in front of the house's north front.

Left: Cusworth's Robert Cecil Battie-Wrightson, pictured with his mother Lady Isabella.

Below: This is reputedly an early picture of Cusworth Park Cricket Team. The date is unknown.

Right: A group of people, presumably friends of the Cusworth Agent, pose outside Dillicar House, from where he operated.

Below: Cusworth Park Cricket Team. In the middle on the back row is Robert Cecil Battie-Wrightson.

Lady Isabella (left), poses for local photographer Luke Bagshaw, *c.* 1910, when the King's Own Yorkshire Light Infantry were provided with afternoon tea. On the right is Anna Maria Middleton, Lady Isabella's companion and a nurse to Robert and Barbara. W.H. Gordon-Smith (1990) mentions that the latter two mischievously nicknamed her 'the cat'.

Lady Isabella on the steps of Cusworth Hall's north front on 22 June 1911, at the time of the celebration of the coronation of King George V. Commenting on the time Lady Isabella spent at Cusworth, W.H. Gordon-Smith states that, 'Despite her mixed fortunes at Cusworth, she had treated her tenants liberally, was charitable to the poor and needy, and a liberal contributor to religious and philanthropic causes. She patronised the trade of the town of Doncaster and took seriously her responsibilities as the controller of large estates'.

Mabel Watson pictured at Levitt Hagg, with No. 1 and the blacksmith's shop in the background.

Members of the Don Valley Field Target Club, holding the first North East Field Target Association Championships in Levitt Hagg during October 1986.

Sledgers enjoying the snow during February 1978 on the field at the side of Levitt Hagg wood.

The Chester family pictured outside No. 6 Levitt Hagg, *c.* 1910. Mrs Elizabeth Chester, middle row, second from the right, acted as unofficial nurse and midwife for the village. She helped many a villager into the world and assisted in their final hours. Elizabeth died, aged 93, on Easter Sunday 1948. Her family donated her wedding dress to Doncaster Museum, now held at Cusworth Hall Museum.

Arthur Harris, Tom Watson's milk roundsman, pictured at Levitt Hagg.

Levitt Hagg quarry workers. At one time the men worked six days a week: five days from 6.00 am to 5.30 pm, with an hour and a half for meals; working seven hours on Saturdays. The picture gives a lengthwise view of the interior of an 'underneath' passage on the rock face. When the pillars on the left were blown away, the 'face', having no support came down, bringing thousands of tons of limestone.

Levitt Hagg quarry workers. From left to right: Geoff Batty, Billy Batty and David Hughes.

Levitt Hagg Cricket Team.

Levitt Hagg quarry worker. It took three months to prepare the rock face for blasting and another three to clear and process the stone. There were a number of faces being worked simultaneously with such names as 'Dartmoor', 'Jackdaw' and 'Primrose'.

Levitt Hagg quarry workers. Left to right: G. Stokes, W. Booth, J. Coggan, F. Booth, G.W. Booth, C. Barker (back), C. Watson, G. Thompson, A. Scrivens, S. Day, J. Barber, W. Thompson, W. Barber.

Above: Levitt Hagg quarry workers.
Those depicted include: Herbert
Smith, Jack Brenan, C. Watson,
Billy Booth (jnr), Bill Chester,
Geoff Batty, Billy Booth, Harry
Pickard, Fred Adams,
Arthur Botterill.

Left: Levitt Hagg quarry workers.
From left to right: J. Hallgate,
C. Barker, L. Birkinshaw, B. Spink,
Wilf Watson, E. Ramsdon.

Lorry driver Wilf Watson at Levitt Hagg Quarry, ready to deliver stone locally by road. Note the lorry's solid wheels and chain-driven back axle.

While this picture is captioned Sprotbrough Donkeys, the animals were actually photographed at Levitt Hagg.

View of the Cusworth gamekeeper with his cottage in the background.

A group of children enjoy having their picture taken, though one of them appears to be bored with the event.

A couple of swells posing for the camera on Sprotbrough Bridge in about 1920.

Above: Another figure group near the River Don at Sprotbrough, c. 1890.

Left: Sir Godfrey Copley, FRS (1653-1709). An engraved portrait by John Smith, after John Zachary Kneller.

Above: Sprotbrough School group. Sprotbrough's old village school was erected around 1840, a house also adjoined for the headmaster. Kelly's *Directory for the West Riding* (1877) mentions the following about the school: 'There is a private school for boys and girls, and a Sunday School held in school house erected by Sir J.W. Copley who pays the salaries of the master and mistress'. In 1912, the *Doncaster Gazette Directory* stated the Sprotbrough School headmaster was W.H. Waterson (from about 1904 to 1924), and his assistants were S.E. Downing and E. Owlett. Sprotbrough School presently occupies another building, opened in 1966.

Right: Brigadier-General Sir Robert Calverley Alington Bewicke-Copley served with the Nile expedition, 1884-5, was with the Chitral relief force, 1895, was in the operations in Kuhram Valley and at the the relief of of Gurlistan 1897, amongst others. He commanded the 17th Infantry Brigade in the Irish Command for three years (1909-12), and retired in the latter year with the honourary rank of Brigadier General. He was an active and valued member of the West Riding Territorial Association and President of the Doncaster and Don Valley Conservative and Unionist Association. He died aged 68 in 1923, the last squire of Sprotbrough.

Lilly Short collecting water from Sprotbrough village pump, situated beneath an impressive coat of arms in a stone alcove.

A corn miller at Sprotbrough, c. 1890.

The water pump at Lower Sprotbrough with Mabel Watson on the left, and Gladys Batty on the right.

Right: Jack Warrender was financial secretary for the Sprotbrough Club and a right arm medium-paced bowler who had his most successful season in 1941 in the Second Division of the Doncaster and District League, when he scored 62 wickets for an average of just over seven.

Below: Sprotbrough Cricket Club, *c.* 1920. Back row: W. Athron, B. Dent, R. McFarlane, W. McFarlane, W. Dent (snr), J. Barker, T. Camm, N. Short. Middle row: W.Dent (jnr), H. Burkinshaw, E. Short, C. Stacey, J. Swainson. Front row: C. Nelson, R. Dent, I. Bower, E. Short, F. Rockliffe.

Above: View of Sprotbrough Flash from Heron Hide, looking towards St Mary's church, Sprotbrough. (Photograph by Hugh Parkin)

Opposite above: Sprotbrough Flash was officially opened on 12 June 1984 by the Chairman of South Yorkshire County Council's Environment Committee, Councillor Ken Willers. The opening ceremony was hosted by the Trust President Joan Duncan, who welcomed the 100 guests and officials representing the three main authorities who were involved in the three year development programme. This programme involved flood control work, footpath development and hide construction with the finances provided by SYCC and the Countryside Commission.

Opposite below: Sprotbrough is the seventh nature reserve managed by the Yorkshire Wildlife Trust within a ten mile radius of Doncaster and is an example of co-operation and co-ordination between the land owners, the British Water Authority (who required the wetland for a flood control washland) and South Yorkshire Environment Department who act as co-ordinators and sponsors. The Trust has also negotiated a wardening agreement with Steetly Minerals covering the adjacent woodland. This and the wetland reserve (totalling some 280 acres) are available for natural history studies. The picture shows Rachel and Daniel from Copley Middle School after the latter responded to an invitation to come up with a title for a hide – Heron Hide – at Sprotbrough Flash. Photograph by Hugh Parkin.

County Councillor Ken Willers (left), Chairman of South Yorkshire County Council Environment Committee is pictured at the official opening ceremony of Sprotbrough Flash Nature Reserve on 12 June 1984, with Hugh Parkin, Chairman of the Reserve's Management Committee. Sprotbrough Flash is a narrow strip of water three-quarters of a mile long, lying alongside the River Don, just upstream from Sprotbrough Lock. It was formed by subsidence about 1924.

The Chairman of South Yorkshire County Council Environment Committee, Cllr Ken Willers, opens Sprotbrough Flash Nature Reserve, accompanied by the Yorkshire Wildlife Trust president, Mrs Joan Duncan. Peter Hardy MP hosted the event in his capacity as patron of the Yorkshire Wildlife Trust. The Yorkshire Water Authority was anxious to retain the lake at Sprotbrough Flash as an area of controlled washland to prevent flooding in the vicinity. Yorkshire Wildlife Trust (formerly the Yorkshire Naturalist Trust) was keen to preserve the water for the wildlife it harboured.

Six

Aerial Views

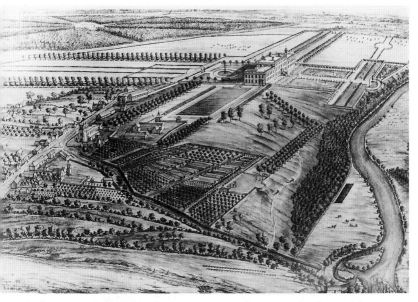

A bird's eye view titled Sprotbrough, near Doncaster, in the County of York, one of the seats of the Hon Sir Godfrey Copley. The view was drawn by Leonard Knyff, born in Haarlem in 1650, who in the late 1690s settled in London, devoting himself to topographical drawings and paintings, becoming known by his series of bird's eye views of the homes of the English gentry and nobility. He died in 1721. The view was engraved by I. Kip.

Above: Aerial view of Sprotbrough from the church tower, looking west, *c.* 1960.

Opposite above: Aerial view of Sprotbrough from the south in 1932.

Opposite below: Aerial view of Sprotbrough looking east, *c.* 1964.

Aerial view of Sprotbrough from the church tower, looking west, *c.* 1960.